CW00891189

Forthcoming titles in this series will include

- *Winning Negotiation Tactics!*
- *Winning CVs!*
- *Getting Hired!*
- *Successful Interviewing Techniques!*
- *Letter Writing for Winners!*
- *Winning Telephone Techniques!*

Do you have any ideas for subjects which could be included in this exciting and innovative series? Could your company benefit from close involvement with a forthcoming title?

Please write to David Grant Publishing Limited
80 Ridgeway, Pembury, Tunbridge Wells, Kent TN2 4EZ
with your ideas or suggestions

PAINLESS BUSINESS FINANCE

Mark Allin

60 Minutes Success Skills Series

Copyright © David Grant Publishing Limited 1998

First published 1998 by
David Grant Publishing Limited
80 Ridgeway
Pembury
Kent TN2 4EZ
United Kingdom

99   98   10 9 8 7 6 5 4 3 2 1

60 Minutes Success Skills Series is an imprint of
David Grant Publishing Limited

British Library Cataloguing in Publication Data
A CIP record for this book is available from the British Library

ISBN 1-901306-05-4

Cover design: Steve Haynes
Text design: Graham Rich
Production editor: Paul Stringer
Typeset in Futura by Archetype IT Ltd,
Cheltenham UK and Camplong d'Aude, France
http://www.archetype-it.com

Printed and bound in Great Britain by
T.J. International, Padstow, Cornwall

This book is printed on acid-free paper

*The publishers accept no responsibility for any investment or financial
decisions made on the basis of the information in this book. Readers are advised
always to consult a qualified financial adviser.*

*All names mentioned in the text have been changed to protect the identity
of the business people involved. Any resemblance to existing companies or people
is entirely coincidental.*

CONTENTS

WELCOME!

ABOUT *PAINLESS BUSINESS FINANCE*

Can you learn how to read and use company accounts as well as picking up sound financial management techniques in just one hour? The answer is a resounding "Yes".

The only bit of waffle in this book

This book is part of the 60 Minutes Success Skills Series. The series is written for people with neither the time nor patience to trawl through acres of jargon, management speak and page-filling waffle. Many people would have you think that business finance is incredibly difficult and that accounts can only be read by obsessive accountants. In fact the principles are very easy and a good understanding of how to use financial information is essential for any manager or business owner.

   This book recognises that time is precious. Like all the books in the series, it is founded on the belief that you can learn all you really need to know quickly and without fuss.

What is business finance?

Business finance refers to the creation and use of company accounts, plans, budgets and reports which are expressed financially as profit and loss accounts, balance sheets and cash flow statements and forecasts. These reports and accounts are used to determine how a company is using its money, whether it is making a profit and to help develop future plans and strategies.

Is this book for you?

Are you:

- ○ *Confused by company accounts?*
- ○ *Mystified by colleagues' discussions of overheads, profit, assets and investment?*
- ○ *Desperate to get promoted but know your lack of financial knowledge is holding you back?*
- ○ *Running or planning to run your own business and need better day-to-day financial management skills?*

If so, you could be one of the many thousands of managers and business people who feel bemused by numbers and finance and think there is no way to learn. Well, help is at hand. In *Painless Business Finance* you will find all you need to know to start tackling financial problems with confidence.

The message in this book is "it's OK to skim". *Painless Business Finance* has been written to dip into, so feel free to flick through it to find the help you most need. To help build your understanding, there are exercises which take you through the steps of building and using accounts. However, if you're really short of time, you can skip straight to the worked examples.

With *Painless Business Finance* in your briefcase you will never be frightened by finances again. Good luck!

What's in this chapter for you

What a balance sheet is
How the balance sheet is put together
What balance sheets can be used for

❝ *My colleagues all seem so at home when the company balance sheet is discussed. I just try to nod in the right places and hope that nobody asks me anything technical.* ❞
– Dennis Miller, regional sales manager

Have you been faced with a balance sheet in a meeting and just felt totally confused, not knowing where to start?

What a balance sheet is

Simply, a balance sheet is a snapshot of the business at a given moment in time (often the end of a financial year or quarter). It shows where the business got its money from and how that money is being used. It shows what the business *owns* (its *assets* – buildings, widgets, cash) and how much it *owes* to other people (its *liabilities*). Like a football league table, the balance sheet shows the state of the teams *today*: it can be totally different from yesterday or tomorrow.

What does the balance sheet show?

❝ *As I'm no accountant, I think of the balance sheet like the freeze frame on a video recorder. It's as if you've stopped the business to look at how the money is being used and what's owed and owing.* ❞
– Ian Wright, Wright Surveyors

> Imagine that somebody had asked you for a loan. How would you assess their financial reliability to check they could be relied on to pay you back? What would you look for?

You'd probably want to know most if not all of the following points about the borrower:

- *How much money that person had in the bank.*
- *What other savings they had.*
- *How much money they owed on their mortgage.*
- *What other loans they had outstanding.*
- *Whether they were owed any money.*
- *How much money they saved after paying all their bills.*

And so on. This would give you a check of that person's all round financial health — what money they have and how they are using and managing it. This is exactly what a balance sheet shows for a business. It is *the* most important measure.

How the balance sheet is put together

> Given that you know the balance sheet is about where a company's money comes from and how it is being used what sort of things would you expect to see on it?

Let's use the example of Rosie's Roses, a new upmarket flower shop in a big city.

Rosie has quit the local LoadsaFlora after a nasty row over petunias. She is determined to go out on her own and has found a vacant shop. Now she needs money. She borrows 5,000 from her father and puts in 5,000 of her own money. Being a sensible person she puts the cash in a charge-free business account at the local bank. Amazingly, she already has a balance sheet!

It looks like this:

Current assets

Cash at bank	10,000	
		10,000

Financed by

Equity		5,000
Loan		5,000
		10,000

> **Assets**: anything of value the business owns for either long-term use (buildings, machinery etc.) called **fixed assets** or for more short-term use (stock, cash, money owed by other people etc.) called **current assets**.
>
> **Equity**: the money that the owners or shareholders have put into the business. It is not paid back – they get their return in dividends and in the growth of the value of the business.

JARGON buster

Now Rosie needs some flowers to sell, some pots and shelves to display them in the shop and a van to deliver them to local customers:

- ○ *she buys 1,000-worth of flowers from Liz's Wholesale on credit;*
- ○ *she buys 500-worth of pots and shelves for cash;*
- ○ *she buys a second-hand van for 4,000 for cash.*

How will this be reflected on the balance sheet?

 YOU?

Now her balance sheet looks like this:

Fixed assets

Van	4,000	
Fittings	500	
		4,500

Current assets

Stock	1,000	
Cash in bank	5,500	
	6,500	

Current liabilities

Liz's Wholesale	1,000	

Current assets minus current liabilities		5,500
		10,000

Capital employed

Equity	5,000	
Loan	5,000	
		10,000

Liabilities: the money, goods or services a business owes.

Liz's Wholesale is a **creditor** – someone the business owes money to.

Remember: the top part shows how the money is being used in a business and how much it owes; the bottom part shows where the money came from. The two halves must balance – which is logical as where else can the money have come from? Either you spent it on more flowers or a leopard-skin steering wheel cover for the van (current or fixed assets) or you still have it (cash – i.e. equity or loan).

If you have stock, this is an asset too as you can sell it. However, you have to pay for it first – hence current liabilities must be deducted from current assets before your balance sheet will balance.

> **Make sure you understand how the balance sheet has been put together so far.**

Now let's complicate matters.

Rosie has finally opened the shop and to her delight has sold something. She sells half of her stock in three days for 1,500 cash, making a profit of 1,000 – that is the sales income (1,500) less the value of half the stock (500).

> **Where does this profit go on the balance sheet? Is it an asset, a liability or a source of finance?**

The profit is part of the funding, of course. The amount of money available to the business has increased, having been introduced by the customers.

> **What else will change on the balance sheet? Remember, Rosie's shifted a lot of roses.**

Let's see:

Fixed assets

Van	4,000	
Fittings	500	
		4,500

Current assets

Stock	500	
Cash in bank	7,000	
	7,500	

Current liabilities

Liz's Wholesale	1,000	

Current assets minus current liabilities		6,500
		11,000

Capital employed

Equity		5,000
Profit		1,000
Loan		5,000
		11,000

Be honest, did you get all that? OK, the stock goes *down* (because Rosie sold it), the cash at the bank goes *up* (because she managed to persuade someone to pay her for the stock). And it all balances because of the 1,000 profit which has been added to the funding.

Remember: if you change anything in the top part of the balance sheet a corresponding change will be needed at the bottom.

❝ *I just try to remember that everything you do seems to have at least two effects on the balance sheet: if you buy stocks on credit your liabilities increase as well as your stocks – if you sell for cash your cash goes up and stocks down and so on...it becomes easier the more you look at it.* **❞**
– Lee Dixon, Dock Green Locks

Now Rosie feels solvent and pays off the money she owes Liz's Wholesale and buys another 3,000-worth of flowers on credit.

One of her early customers works for a big local insurance company and is so impressed she recommends Rosie as the firm's main supplier of flowers for the boardroom and reception. They order 1,500-worth of flowers (again at a profit of 1,000) but, being a big company, they insist on credit which Rosie gives them.

Rosie has also bought 100-worth of seeds and planted them to produce her own stock. She also pays her first 200 in rent on the shop.

Now how does the balance sheet look? Where will the 1,500 of credit go? And the planted seeds? And the rent?

Fixed assets

Van	4,000	
Fittings	500	
		4,500

Current assets

Stock	3,000	
Work in progress	100	
Debtors	1,500	
Cash in bank	5,700	
	10,300	

Current liabilities

Liz's Wholesale	3,000	

Current assets minus current liabilities		7,300
		11,800

Capital employed

Equity	5,000	
Profit	1,800	
Loan	5,000	
		11,800

So, the seeds are work in progress. The 1,500 credit becomes an asset because it is money which the business is *owed* and if necessary could claim. The rent is an expense so must be deducted from the profit.

> **Work in progress:** *goods which are in the process of being made ready for sale but are not yet finished goods. You might also see raw materials under assets (like stocks of cloth for a clothing manufacturer).*

JARGON buster

Note: The profit figure on a balance sheet is often listed as *profit and loss account* or *retained earnings* and is the profit figure from the P&L carried over – it is not worked out each time as we have done here.

Why is it not the same as a profit and loss account?

A profit and loss account shows the income (from sales) and expenses (materials, salaries etc.) for a business during the whole of a given period and shows whether or not the company has made a profit or loss and how much. It is **not** the same as a balance sheet! P&Ls are covered in the next chapter.

What balance sheets can be used for

So, we now have a balance sheet at the end of Rosie's Roses' first three weeks of business. What does it tell us about that business?

Think about what you might use a balance sheet for if you were a manager in a firm or a bank manager or a potential acquirer. Write down some of your ideas.

ACT!

The balance sheet can be used to answer some important questions:

○ *How much money does the business **owe** compared with how much it is **owed**?*
○ *How quickly is it paid by its debtors?*
○ *Does it have sufficient funds to pay its creditors?*
○ *Does it have enough stock to meet demand?*

> ❝ *I use the balance sheet of a firm like a doctor's report. More than the P&L, it tells me if the company is healthy, how long it has to live, what kind of medicine it needs.* ❞
> **– Colin Francis, management consultant**

When things go wrong

Let's think about a different business. Full Optics is a firm manufacturing high-specification lenses for optical equipment. It has raised 100,000 of investment and has numerous lucrative on-going government contracts. It has expensive machinery and an impressive head office. In its first year it just broke even but things are looking better at the end of the second as two big new contracts have been won, for delivery in three years' time. However, the firm needed a loan to tool up for the work.

Here's the company's simplified balance sheet at the end of year two:

Fixed assets

Machinery	44,000	
		44,000

Current assets

Stock	50,000
Work in progress	2,000
Debtors	240,000
Cash in bank	31,000
	323,000

Current liabilities

Creditors	241,000

Current assets minus current liabilities		82,000
		126,000

Capital employed

Equity	100,000
Profit	1,000
Loan	25,000
	126,000

> **So, what is your assessment of Rosie's Roses and Full Optics given the balance sheets for the two businesses?**

The balance sheet tells us a lot about liquidity (i.e. whether the company can afford to pay its bills). Let's use two simple but powerful ratios to understand exactly what is going on in each business, then become financial management consultants overnight, leave our jobs, earn a fortune and retire in five years!

1. Current ratio

Current ratio = current assets ÷ current liabilities

This ratio should not normally fall below about 1.5 (i.e. the company should have enough cash to pay its debts and still have half as much again left over). If it is lower than 1.0, the value of the assets is not enough to cover the liabilities.

So, for Rosie's Roses:

   $10,300 ÷ 3,000 = 3.3$

And for Full Optics:

   $323,000 ÷ 241,000 = 1.3$

2. Quick ratio

Quick ratio = (current assets − stock) ÷ current liabilities

This ratio shows the money you can lay your hands on relatively quickly (it should not really be below 1).

So, for Rosie's Roses:

$$7,300 \div 3,000 = 2.43$$

And for Full Optics:

$$273,000 \div 241,000 = 1.13$$

> **Both of these ratios show us whether the company has assets in excess of its liabilities (i.e. whether it can pay its bills).**

Rosie's Roses looks to be in a strong position and can pay its creditors easily. But is it really making best use of the capital it has? Does it have enough stock? What if a big order comes in?

Full Optics appears in a weaker position but it is owed a lot of money. Can it speed up its payments? Is it underfunded? After all, governments are slow payers but they are good for the money.

> *In the early years we used the balance sheet to check we were liquid – it helps you step back from the day-to-day stuff and look at the big picture. Can we really pay our bills over time? Can we get hold of the cash we are owed if we need it? It's about good management but the financial reports give you what you need to make decisions.*
> **– David Rogers, Rogers Publishing**

Reading a balance sheet is common sense. Once you know how it is put together and what the elements are then ratios will help but good business sense will be more useful.

After finishing this book get hold of the balance sheet for your business. Use it to assess the position your company is in. If you have time try to draw up a balance sheet for another business using the blank sheet opposite. Take the following information as your starting point.

Bertie's Booze Bazaar is a ramshackle but inviting specialist wine store near the financial district of the city. Here is the story of his first three months. Draw up a balance sheet for the end of the whole period and decide if it's a business you would invest in!

○ **Month 1**: *Bertie raises 35,000 of equity and puts it in the bank. He finds premises at 400 per month and buys 15,000-worth of stock from St Ringer Inc., a wine wholesaler, half on credit, and 500-worth of fittings for the shop.*

○ **Month 2**: *Bertie sells all his stock, half for cash and half on credit, at a 100% profit! He buys another 20,000 of stock on credit and some ornate wine racks for the shop for 2,000 cash. He spends 1,000 on an advertisement in the local newspaper.*

○ **Month 3**: *Bertie sells another half of his stock on credit at 7,000 profit following the advert. He places three more ads for 500 each and hires an assistant at 500 per month. He buys a van for 5,000. He buys another 10,000 of stock but is asked to pay 50% of the existing debt first, which he does. He unsuccessfully chases his debtors for payment.*

Fixed assets

Van

Fittings

_____

Current assets

Stock

Debtors

Cash

_____

Current liabilities

Creditors

_____

Current assets minus current liabilities

_____

Capital employed

Equity

Profit

Loan

_____

Bertie's balance sheet looks like this:

Fixed assets

Van	5,000	
Fittings	2,500	
		7,500

Current assets

Stock	20,000	
Debtors	32,000	
Cash in bank	17,050	
	69,050	

Current liabilities

St Ringer Inc.	23,750	

Current assets minus current liabilities		45,300
		52,800

Capital employed

Equity		35,000
Profit		17,800
Loan		0
		52,800

Did it balance for you? (If not make sure you subtracted all the expenses from the profit figure – rent, advertising and wages – and that you reduced the cash figure as well.)

What conclusions did you reach about the business?

❍ *Is the stock level too high/OK/too low?*
❍ *Can the bills be paid?*
❍ *Is he being paid quickly enough?*

Using the current and quick ratios shows that Bertie is doing well.

Balance sheet basics:

1. Think of the balance sheet as a snapshot which gives a picture of a firm's all-round financial health.
2. It shows where the money comes from in a business (loan, equity, profits) and how it is used (cash, stock, plant).
3. It is NOT the same as a P&L.
4. Balance sheets can be used to determine whether a company has too much stock, has trouble paying its bills, receives money too slowly.

What's in this chapter for you

Understanding the profit and loss account
Constructing a P&L
Managing different kinds of costs
Using the P&L to manage profitability

> " *Everyone talks about profit, profit, profit but I don't really know how its calculated or even what it is for my firm.* "
> – **Paul Farr, St Ringer Inc.**

Imagine a colleague asks you "what is the P&L implication of this decision?" Do you feign an acute attack of laryngitis rather than answer?

What is a profit and loss account?

The profit and loss account (let's call it the P&L, everyone else does) shows the sales revenue, cost of sales, overheads and profit or loss for a business over a given period, say a quarter or a year. It provides managers, shareholders and the bank with the vital information about whether the business is profitable and what sort of return is being generated on the capital employed in the business (more about that later).

Remember: the balance sheet is a snapshot of the health of the business at one point in time; the P&L shows income and expenditure over a given length of time. Cash flow statements show the flow of actual money in and out of the business and are different again (you'll be pleased to know) but are covered later.

The basics of the P&L

What is profit? "Dumb question," you might think. So, what is it? Write down your definition.

There are four basic elements in the P&L:

○ *Sales income*
○ *Cost of sales*
○ *Overheads*
○ *Net profit/loss.*

Here comes a very easy but really rather important formula, so don't forget it.

$$Profit = sales\ income - cost\ of\ sales - overheads$$

So, there we have it – that's what profit is. Of course, you knew it all along!

JARGON buster

Cost of sales: *the cost to you of purchasing the goods you sell, whether that is buying finished goods or buying raw materials with which to manufacture your product.*

Overheads: *the running costs of a business – the biggest are usually premises and people. These are fixed regardless of the level of sales – you can't move offices from week to week depending on sales!*

For an automobile manufacturer, are the following items overheads or cost of sales?

	OVERHEAD	COST OF SALES
○ MD's salary		
○ tyres		
○ sales commission		
○ sheet metal		
○ transporter trucks		
○ computers		
○ spark plugs		

> If you are thinking too hard, remember: something which would represent the same cost to the company regardless of the number of cars sold is an overhead (salary, computers, transport); something which becomes a greater or lesser cost depending on how many are sold is a cost of sale (all raw materials, sales commissions, distribution charges).

❝ *Until I understood the difference between overheads and cost of sales I was misinterpreting all the advice I was getting from the bank and the accountants. They really are very different and are managed in very different ways.* ❞
– Denis Newton, marketing consultant

Putting together the P&L

Let's go back to Rosie's Roses and build up a P&L for the business.

The story so far:

- ○ Rosie borrows 5,000 from her father and puts in 5,000 of her own money.
- ○ She buys 1,000-worth of flowers from Liz's Wholesale on credit.
- ○ She buys 500-worth of pots and shelves for cash.
- ○ She buys a second-hand van for 4,000 for cash.
- ○ She sells half of her initial stock in three days for 1,500 cash.
- ○ Now Rosie feels solvent and pays off the 1,000 she owes Liz's Wholesale.
- ○ She buys another 3,000-worth of flowers on credit.
- ○ A local insurance firm orders 1,500-worth of flowers (again at a profit of 1,000) but, being a big company, insists on credit, which Rosie gives them.
- ○ Rosie has also bought 100-worth of seeds and planted them to produce her own stock.
- ○ She also pays her first 200 rent on the shop.

> Before we put together the P&L, think through which of these are overheads and which are cost of sales.

The P&L would look like this:

Sales		3,000
Cost of sales		
Opening stock	0	
Purchases	4,100	
Closing stock	3,100	
Cost of goods sold		1,000
Gross profit		2,000
Overheads		
Rent		200
Net profit		1,800

Sales income: the value of the flowers sold in the period in question (1,500 cash, 1,500 credit) *regardless* of whether she was actually paid for them in this period or not.

Cost of sales: the cost to Rosie of those flowers sold (2 × 500), *not* of the total purchases made. For companies which manufacture their products this would be the cost of the raw materials and the cost of making them into whatever they are selling. For a business like Rosie's it is the cost of buying the product which is then sold on.

Overheads: the cost of rent. Obviously over a full year Rosie would have many more expenses than this – she might pay herself a salary, she would need to put petrol in the van, she will need an accountant, she might have part-time help. All of these expenses for the business are included in the P&L as overheads.

This is a very simple example but contains all the main features of the P&L which would be exactly the same for a much larger business.

The Balance Sheet and P&L together

Remember: we are only looking at the sales made in a particular period and the cost of those sales. Some of the purchases Rosie has in stock might be sold in the period after this one or the one after that. So, the closing stock is subtracted from the opening stock and gives us the value of goods sold in the period. So what about the unsold purchases – where are they? *On the balance sheet* as an asset (something the business owns).

And what about the van? Where is that? It's also *on the balance sheet*. It is an asset, meaning that it might generate money for the business in the future if Rosie sells it but is not a cost of sale in this year.

You need both accounts to get the full picture of a business. The P&L won't tell you if the business is buying too much stock just to get costs down and increase profits – but the balance sheet will because the stocks would be high. The balance sheet won't tell you if the business is generating profits on every sale – the P&L will.

Depreciation

Let's get back to the van. If Rosie (or more likely her accountant) thinks she won't get the full 4,000 for it if she sold it, the van is *depreciated*. If it is worth only 3,000 then it is reduced to that amount on the balance sheet and 1,000 is put on to the P&L as an expense.

Depreciation: *the reduction in value of an asset on the balance sheet. The amount of the reduction is charged to the P&L as an expense.*

Have a look at the P&L for Rosie's Roses. If the van was to be depreciated by 1,000 the profit would be reduced to 800 and on the balance sheet on page 16 the asset value would go down to 3,000 and the profit figure at the bottom would be reduced by 1,000 so it will still balance.

> **❝** *Until our financial director talked me through the P&L I never truly realised what the costs of the business are. Now I am much happier managing the costs of my team and I don't suffer nearly so much bullying by the accountants!* **❞**
> **– Gary Cluny, healthcare manager**

Now it's your turn! Remember Bertie's Booze Bazaar from chapter 1? Construct the P&L for Bertie's first quarter using the blank template opposite. Looking back at the balance sheet on page 24 will help.

Here's a reminder of the story so far:

○ **Month 1:** *Bertie raises 35,000 of equity and puts it in the bank. He finds premises at 400 per month and buys 15,000-worth of stock from St Ringer Inc., a wine wholesaler, half on credit, and 500-worth of fittings for the shop.*

○ **Month 2:** *Bertie sells all his stock, half for cash and half on credit, at a 100% profit! He buys another 20,000 of stock on credit and some ornate wine racks for the shop for 2,000 cash. He spends 1,000 on an advertisement in the local newspaper.*

○ **Month 3:** *Bertie sells another half of his stock on credit at 7,000 profit following the advert. He places three more ads for 500 each and hires an assistant at 500 per month. He buys a van for 5,000. He buys another 10,000 of stock but is asked to pay 50% of the existing debt first, which he does. He unsuccessfully chases his debtors for payment.*

Sales   47,000

Cost of sales

Opening stock   0

Purchases   45,000

Closing stock   20,000

Cost of goods sold   25,000
                                                          _____
Gross profit   22,000

Overheads

Rent   1,200

Marketing   2,500

Salaries   500
                            _____   _____
                                                              4,200

Net profit

The P&L should look like this:

Sales		47,000
Cost of sales		
Opening stock	0	
Purchases	45,000	
Closing stock	20,000	
Cost of goods sold		<u>25,000</u>
Gross profit		22,000
Overheads		
Rent	1,200	
Marketing	2,500	
Salaries	<u>500</u>	
		4,200
Net profit		17,800

The profit figure would go over to the balance sheet as retained earnings. Remember: the van and fittings are assets and do not appear anywhere on the P&L unless they are depreciated.

VERY IMPORTANT TIP

❏ *PROFIT is not the same as CASH (even though big businesses in particular seem to think it is). You can have a paper profit but no cash if your customers pay late or if you have invested heavily in balance sheet items like furniture, expensive cars etc. When looking at company accounts, head for the cash figure first. Is it enough to pay the creditors if needs be? Is it a good proportion of the profit figure (like 30% or more)? Has it gone up since last year? This may well tell you more than the "bottom line".*

Using the P&L

> ❝ *The monthly P&L is the hottest item at our management meetings. We us it to plan the next month, control our costs, and set new sales targets.* ❞
> **– Roy Lawrence, direct marketer**

The P&L is used to measure and manage profitability. Managers use it to:

○ *analyse where the major costs are and if necessary reduce them;*
○ *see if costs are increasing or decreasing as a percentage of sales or profits (they should not increase, of course, but a significant decline might highlight underinvestment);*
○ *identify areas for reducing expenditure;*
○ *identify areas for increasing investment;*
○ *see how profits are moving quarter on quarter and year on year.*

Using the numbers

Now we are going to use some very simple ratios to show how the P&L can be used to manage the business:

$$Net\ margin = (net\ profit \div sales) \times 100$$

This is the basic profit figure after all costs but usually before tax. For Bertie's Booze Bazaar it is 38% ([17,800 ÷ 47,000] ×100) which is very good. In general it should be between 10 and 20% but there are no hard and fast rules. It depends how *much* profit is generated (50% of not much is very little!). It is also important to look at how it changes from period to period. It might also be higher in some industries (accountancy, arms manufacturing) than others (supermarkets, freelance editing).

$$Gross\ margin = (gross\ profit \div sales) \times 100$$

This is a quick way of looking at how high your cost of sales is. Bertie comes in at 47% ([22,000 ÷ 47,000] × 100). What is important here is the level of overheads because they are pretty much fixed. If you know your overheads average 60% of sales and you want a net margin of 10% then you are going to need a gross margin of 70%. If you aren't there, you can look at reducing cost of sales by smarter negotiating, new suppliers, cheaper materials etc. This can be an easier and quicker solution than tampering with overheads, which usually means getting rid of people. Whilst this might be a positive boon in the case of certain people in your company it is to be frowned upon if a business is to grow.

$$Return\ on\ investment = (profit^* \div assets^{**}) \times 100$$

*before interest and tax; **or capital employed

"Hang on," you might think, "this uses both accounts – balance sheet and the P&L!" Right you are. We've already said they were inseparable and a true picture of a business must look at both. The return on investment (ROI) is perhaps the best measure of profitability and return, showing how the business is providing a return on the money put into it not just on this year's expenditure. For Bertie it is:

(17,800 ÷ 52,800) × 100 = 34%

This is again very good. The acceptable range is roughly from 10% to 30%, though a venture capitalist might well look for a lot more. One thing's for certain, it must be positive or things will look bleak for the survival of the business.

❝ *We use gross and net profit ratios as quick measures of how the business is doing over time. If the ratio has worsened or improved from one quarter to another it can tell you things the numbers alone cannot. As tools for checking the company's progress, they are invaluable.* ❞
– Nicky Norman, Norm's Gnomes

The basics of P&Ls

1. The P&L is a picture of the profitability of a business over a given period.
2. Profit = sales income – cost of sales – overheads
   Sales = the sales made in that year (not cash)
   Cost of sales = the cost of producing the goods sold (not all the goods made or purchased).
3. Overheads and cost of sales are different costs and must be managed differently.
4. Profit is **not** the same as cash.
5. Ratios can provide a quick way of using the information on the P&L to manage income and costs effectively.

What's in this chapter for you

> *Understanding cash flow*
> *Managing cash*
> *Forecasting cash movements*

> ❝ *It's always the same. These young entrepreneurs have a great idea, sell it brilliantly, get all cocky – and then run out of money! When will they learn?* ❞
> **– Roy Evans, accountant**

How often do you worry about cash flow at work? When it comes to your personal finances do you worry about anything else? Chances are that if you run a small business you will have turned straight to this chapter. If you work in a larger business you might wonder what it is doing here. Why is that?

What is cash flow?

Cash flow is the change in a company's cash balance over a period, say a quarter or a year. Let's look at Rosie's Roses. Here is the story again:

- ○ Rosie borrows 5,000 from her father and puts in 5,000 of her own money.
- ○ She buys 1,000-worth of flowers from Liz's Wholesale on credit.
- ○ She buys 500-worth of pots and shelves for cash.
- ○ She buys a second-hand van for 4,000 for cash.
- ○ She sells half of her initial stock in three days for 1,500 cash.
- ○ Now Rosie feels solvent and pays off the 1,000 she owes Liz's Wholesale.
- ○ She buys another 3,000-worth of flowers on credit.
- ○ A local insurance firm orders 1,500-worth of flowers (again at a profit of 1,000) but, being a big company, insists on credit, which Rosie gives them.
- ○ Rosie has also bought 100-worth of seeds and planted them to produce her own stock.
- ○ She also pays her first 200 rent on the shop.

Now work out how much money Rosie has in the bank at the beginning and the end of the period. (Can you think of a quick way of doing it?)

It looks like this:

Opening balance	10,000
Cash inflow	
Sales	1,500
Cash outflow	
Stock	1,000
Materials	100
Rent	200
Van	4,000
Fittings	500
Net flow	−4,300
Closing balance	5,700

Opening balance: the amount of money in the bank at the start of the period.

Cash inflow: money actually received from customers (or in the form of a loan or equity) – not total sales made.

Cash outflow: money paid out to suppliers or for overheads – not cost of sales or invoices received.

Net flow: cash inflow minus cash outflow.

Closing balance: the amount of money in the bank at the end of the period calculated as the opening balance plus net flow. This figure is carried over as the opening balance of the next period.

The "*closing balance*" figure is the same as the "*cash at bank*" figure on the end of period balance sheet on page 16. (This would have been the quick way to do it – surely, though, you didn't cheat!)

So, Rosie's cash flow is minus 4,300. If you got that wrong look carefully at what was bought and sold on credit. Cash flow concerns itself only with the *actual* payment and receipt of cash, not the placing of an order, making of a sale or receipt or issue of invoice.

Cash flow is **not the same as profit** (heard that before?). In an extreme example a company might make a very profitable sale to a single customer which represents 75% of its sales for the year. The P&L will look great – cost of sales will be low (lots of sales to one customer is a "good thing") – then the customer goes bust. Of course, the company can claim on the assets through the receiver but there is no guarantee of getting anything and it could take months or years anyway. Exit one very profitable company.

❝ *I used to tell the bank manager the cash flow was great – we'd sold this much to customer X and this much to customer Y. Whenever I did, his facial expression always dissolved into a mixture of exasperation and pity – now I know why.* ❞
– Steve Cruikshank, builders' merchant

Why is cash flow so important?

This should be self-evident – cash flow determines whether a business has sufficient cash to invest in the raw materials, salaries and other costs necessary to achieve its sales and profits. In the end, a business that continually runs a negative cash flow and therefore does not generate more cash over time than is invested in it is not going to be around for long.

Forecasting cash flow

An understanding of cash flow is vital in forecasting how your business is developing and what it will need in the short and long term.

Let's go back to Rosie's Roses and move the story on a little. Rosie has had a good first three months. She has sold all of her stock and has 2,000 in the bank. The bank manager keeps telling her to plan but she never seems to have the time. Eventually she steels herself and, armed with her three months' experience, writes down a picture of how the business might look over the next month.

sales through shop	*2000*
sales to companies	*2000 (half on thirty days' credit)* *Profit margin on sales to companies not as good as in shop*
stock required	*1500 (half on thirty days' credit)*
rent	*200*
petrol	*75*

Her cash flow forecast would look like this:

Opening balance	2,000
Cash inflow	
Sales	3,000
Cash outflow	
Stock	750
Rent	200
Petrol	150
Net flow	1,900
Closing balance	3,900

Having looked at one month, and consequently feeling confident, Rosie decides to look forward for the next six months and makes some assumptions:

○ *Sales will be 4,000 per month for the first four months and 5,000 for the last two, half made for cash, a quarter on thirty days' credit to the insurance company and a quarter on sixty days' to the local undertaker who insists on these terms if she is to get the business.*

○ *1,500 a month of stock will be needed for the first four months and 2,000 for the last two, half paid for in cash and half on thirty days' credit.*

○ *She has to have a computer for sales letters, accounts etc. and has found a good one for 3,750. Luckily she has plenty in the bank at the moment.*

○ *To expand sales, an advertisement will be placed every week in the local newspaper. This will cost 75 per advert, with payment up front.*

○ *Some help in the shop is needed two mornings a week at 150 per week.*

○ *Rosie needs to take 500 a month out of the business for herself.*

○ *Rent will be 200 per month and petrol 150.*

What will the cash flow look like over the next six months? Work it out using the blank statement provided. Remember: she will still be owed some money and owe some from the month she has just forecast.

Month	1	2	3	4	5	6
Opening balance						
Cash inflow						
Sales						
Cash outflow						
Stock						
Advertising						
Computer						
Salary						
Rosie						
Rent						
Petrol						
Net flow						
Closing balance						

It looks like this:

Month	1	2	3	4	5	6
Opening balance	3,900	−100	−350	400	1,150	2,150
Cash inflow						
Sales	3,000	3,000	4,000	4,000	4,500	4,750
Cash outflow						
Stock	1,500	1,500	1,500	1,500	1,750	2,000
Advertising	300	300	300	300	300	300
Computer	3,750					
Salary	600	600	600	600	600	600
Rosie	500	500	500	500	500	500
Rent	200	200	200	200	200	200
Petrol	150	150	150	150	150	150
Net flow	−4,000	−250	750	750	1,000	1,000
Closing balance	−100	−350	400	1,150	2,150	3,150

Look carefully at how it is put together. Income and expenses take account of when Rosie expects to get paid or pay her suppliers.

Rosie is seriously alarmed. Even though she has put a decent amount of money into the business and knows it is breaking even on sales, she will spend two months in the red and has not agreed an overdraft with the bank.

She then looks at what would happen if sales fell by only 10% (always possible) and is even more alarmed. Furthermore the insurance company has a tendency to pay late and it is quite likely the 3,000 sales in month 3 will become 2,000 meaning a negative flow of over 1,000! Obviously, the computer is a problem but she has to have it and thought she had enough money in the bank to cover it.

Jot down what advice you would give Rosie.

Some suggestions might be:

- Defer the buying of the computer for a month and try to pay on credit.
- Negotiate better credit terms with Liz's Wholesale.
- Offer a small discount to the insurance company and the undertaker if they pay within seven days of invoice.
- Talk to the bank about an overdraft.

A cash flow forecast would enable Rosie to go and see the bank manager with good information. She can show that she will be generating positive cash flows in the near future and that her business is fundamentally profitable but, like many others, has a short-term cash shortfall.

" Our cash flow problems started when we began to grow. Suddenly we had more customers, so more bad debts; we needed to pay out for more equipment and so on. By careful forecasting we were able to see where the problems were and focus on those things we could actually do to improve cash flow. "
– Neil Rudd, CNP Security Services

The balance sheet and cash flow forecast together

Let's look at Rosie's balance sheet for end of the same period. Although she plans carefully she has 1,000-worth of stock still to move out.

Fixed assets

Computer	3,750	
Van	4,000	
Fittings	500	
		8,250

Current assets

Stock	1,000	
Work in progress	100	
Debtors	4,750	
Cash in bank	3,150	
	9,000	

Current liabilities

Liz's Wholesale	1,000	

Current assets minus current liabilities		8,000
		16,250

Capital employed

Equity	5,000
Profit	6,250
Loan	5,000
	16,250

The cash flow statement and balance sheet tell us the *working capital* that is needed in the business.

Working capital *is the day-to-day cash requirement of the business to fund the difference between the time when stocks are paid for and the time when customers pay.*

Working capital is usually calculated as:

stock + work in progress + debtors – liabilities

So for Rosie it is:

(1,000 + 100 + 4,750) – 1,100 = 3,650

This is what is needed to fund the business until the stock is turned into sales and the sales are turned into cash. If the working capital and cash flow position show that the company is going to have trouble meeting its liabilities and day-to-day costs like salaries and rent, remedial action must be taken.

What things could be done to improve working capital?

Here are some possibilities:

Improve payments from customers (credit control)

- ○ *Offer discounts for prompt payment.*
- ○ *Try to do more business with customers who pay well.*
- ○ *Avoid doing business with bad payers.*
- ○ *Employ a factoring company who will pay you a percentage of the invoices you are owed and then take responsibility for collecting the cash.*

Pay suppliers more slowly

This should not be done simply by delaying payment of invoices – the supplier may refuse to supply you, blacklist you, take you to court, and it will certainly ruin your relationship with them! Instead:

- ○ *Try to negotiate better terms with the suppliers, perhaps in return for guaranteeing them regular orders or by making them your major or sole supplier.*
- ○ *Always be on the lookout for new, cheaper suppliers. It is amazing how many business relationships are just habit.*
- ○ *There may be discounts on offer to you for prompt payment. Look at these seriously as they can be very attractive.*

Stock management

How quickly are stocks selling? Do you have dead stock tying up cash?

- ○ *A useful ratio is:*

    cost of sales ÷ stock

    So for Rosie invoiced sales (i.e. not cash received) of 26,000 divided by the closing stock of 1,000 gives a ratio of 26. So, the stock turns over 26 times in the period which is good and right for a shop selling perishables. If this is too low then stock might need to be reduced. Better sales planning can help plan stock requirements. It might also be possible to negotiate quicker delivery times from suppliers to help order only the stock you know you can sell.
- ○ *If you have dead stock look at selling it off cheaply. Better to get your money back than lose it for ever.*

○ *Examine carefully which lines are selling and which aren't. Do you have appropriate stocks of each?*

If all these measures still leave you with a cash shortfall the business may need more capital to fund profitable sales or may, of course, be trading unprofitably. If it is the former then a detailed cash flow forecast will be essential to negotiate an overdraft with the bank.

> **❝** *We are always looking at our working capital position. It takes about four months for us to tool up, produce and sell a product so we need to know we are funded over that period.* **❞**
> **– David James, Creative Plastics**

Cash flow basics

1. Cash flow is the change in a company's cash balance over a set period, say a quarter or a year.
2. Cash is not the same as profit.
3. A cash flow forecast is essential to determine the business's cash requirements.
4. Working capital is the amount needed to fund the gap between paying for new stock and receiving the cash for selling it.
5. The working capital and cash position can be improved by looking at when cash is received from customers, when suppliers have to be paid, how much stock is held and by negotiating an overdraft or injecting more money into the business as a loan or in the form of equity.

What's in this chapter for you

Putting together a sales and costs budget
Thinking about sales and prices
Using the budget to make the right decisions

" *We never budget. We don't need to – and we can't.*
Our business is too fast and dynamic for that. Budgeting is for
accountants and wimps. "
– Gerry Rousset, Snappy Software

Do you think of budget time as the worst part of the year? A
pointless bureaucratic exercise? No relevance to the real
business? WRONG!

Planning ahead

All successful businesses are looking to the future all the time.
There are always new opportunities for growth, new markets, new
products, new customers. New ideas usually cost money and
often require capital expenditure on new machinery, production
methods, premises etc.

Capital Expenditure is money spent on new **fixed assets** (see
chapter 1), often known by your friendly Finance Director as
"capex". These assets will become part of the balance sheet.

JARGON
buster

Many businesses large and small consider the future to be so
unknown that they never plan at all. They simply react to things
when they happen like the arrival of new competitors, cost
increases, new taxes. This can be successful if you have a business
which can move very quickly but most can't (though many
business people think they are the exception). Think how long it
really takes you to get a new product to market – this is your
reaction time.

It makes much more sense to prepare a budget. This makes your plans clear and expresses them financially, using your knowledge of cash flow, balance sheets and profit and loss accounts.

JARGON buster

A **budget** *shows a company's plan for the future in financial terms. It details expected: revenues and sales; costs; profits; and investments.*

Why bother to budget?

❝ *The budget is king for us. We have so many different lines and products that if we didn't plan ahead we would be in real trouble. It is hard work but it gives us all something to go for.* ❞
– **Les Ramsey, toy manufacturer**

There are obvious advantages to budgeting. What would they be for your business?

Some of the benefits of budgeting might be:

- ○ *To help plan monthly cash flows better.*
- ○ *To identify new investment needs in machinery or other assets.*
- ○ *To determine staff levels needed.*
- ○ *To control costs month to month (or day to day!).*
- ○ *To motivate everyone.*

The latter two are very important. If you work in a bigger business you probably hate budget time more than any other. You have to forecast sales (you never guess, of course, not with your experience and business insight), justify costs, fight for resources and so on. But without the budget how would you know if a particular cost incurred during the year was too high or too low? The budget is the only way of putting today's costs in the context of your expected future revenues.

The sales half of the budget gives everybody in the business something to aim for. If the business is to grow these are the sales which have to be achieved. Often these budgets will be used to create individual targets and bonuses.

How do budgets work?

Let's use an example from Bertie's Booze Bazaar. Bertie, as well as having an encyclopaedic knowledge of the world's wines is always on the lookout for new ideas and new business opportunities. He has noticed that his line of new world wines is going particularly well and that his home delivery service is also popular. He sees an advert in the local paper offering the assets of a direct mail company for sale. He goes along and finds out that for 45,000 he could pick up a decent lorry, a franking and packing line, computer system and basic warehouse shelving at the auction in six weeks. He has space at the back of the shop to use. Now is the time for him to pour an industrial-strength gin and tonic and ponder whether it's a *good* proposition.

Bertie spends a month talking to his customers and suppliers as well as people running other direct mail businesses. He decides there is sufficient merit in the idea to take it very seriously. There *is* a market for good unusual wine delivered to your door. Having discarded the name *Basket Cases (mad wine at mad prices)* he has to make some assumptions about *New World Direct*.

Costs and prices

Using his intimate knowledge of what people will *really* pay for wine Bertie works out the following sales for each of four possible prices:

Selling price	7.99	8.49	8.99	9.99
Sales	15,000	14,000	13,000	12,000
Revenue	119,850	118,860	116,870	119,880

He then looks at his costs:

○ *The cost of importing will be 6.00 per bottle for 12,000 but it goes down by 1.00 for each additional thousand up to 15,000.*
○ *He will need to spend 10,000 on brochures and the same again on mailing them.*
○ *Overnight deliveries on the lorry would cost 400 per month.*
○ *Mail deliveries will be 100 per month.*
○ *He will need a packing person, a driver and a marketing manager at 30,000 per year.*

○ *Additional light, electricity and other costs will be 5,000 per year.*

Selling price	7.99	8.49	8.99	9.99
Sales	15,000	14,000	13,000	12,000
Revenue	119,850	118,860	116,870	119,880
Costs	106,000	117,000	126,000	133,000

Now he knows that his total annual overheads are 61,000 (all of the costs above except the van and machinery which are *not* overheads – we'll come to this in the next chapter) on top of the costs of importing for each different quantity in his chart.

The higher price might look the most attractive on the revenue front BUT. . .
. . . Bertie knows that his overheads are 61,000. At the higher price he is netting 3.99 a bottle so he needs to sell 61,000 ÷ 3.99 to break even (cover his costs and overheads) which is over 15,000 bottles – too many at that price! But at the lower price he makes 4.99 per bottle so his break-even is 12,222. This is a *very* important calculation – can you sell enough at a given price to cover costs? If not, forget it.

So he goes for 7.99, 15,000 bottles in year one at a cost of 3.00 per bottle. He also projects forward to show what he expects sales to look like in the next five years:

Yr 1	15,000 bottles
Yr 2	20,000
Yr 3	25,000
Yr 4	27,500
Yr 5	30,000

Use the blank opposite to work out the first year P&L.

Sales

Cost of sales

Opening stock

Purchases

Closing stock

Cost of goods sold

Gross profit

Overheads

Advertising

Salaries

Light etc.

Mail

Van deliveries

Net profit

The P&L looks like this:

Sales		119,850
Cost of sales		
Opening stock	0	
Purchases	60,000	
Closing stock	15,000	
Cost of goods sold		45,000
Gross profit		74,850
Overheads		
Advertising	20,000	
Salaries	30,000	
Light etc.	5,000	
Mail	1,200	
Van deliveries	4,800	
		61,000
Net profit		13,850

If Bertie's sales projections are right then he has a profitable new venture! Of course, from the same figures he would also do a balance sheet and cash flow forecast as outlined in chapters 1 and 3.

Let's look at the principal areas of the P&L budget.

Sales

This is the big one. Everything else (costs, investments, sanity, heart attacks) comes from the sales budget. Is it accurate and achievable? Or is it so high as to be impossible and de-motivating, or so low as to represent no growth or ambition? It is not the aim of this book to show how to create accurate sales forecasts. It takes a combination of experience, prudence and nerve. *However* if a budget is not working (i.e. is not profitable) resist the temptation to jack up the sales. If this is your sales forecast any adjustment to it is likely to combine equal measures of fantasy and bravado. Stay real!

Purchases

Be careful also in predicting the likely cost of sales. Factors which could affect it are:

○ *inflation*
○ *the terms offered by your suppliers*
○ *cash flow (if it's tight you may have to hold fewer stocks which could then cost you more)*
○ *raw materials price increases*
○ *exchange rate fluctuations.*

And so on. Needless to say just using last year's figures is very dangerous.

Overheads

This is often where the big arguments are. New members of staff, increased marketing spend, bigger offices – this is what we all want! As ever there are arguments on both sides but issues to consider are:

○ *What percentage of sales are overheads, compared with last year?*
○ *Overheads should rarely increase as a percentage unless you are investing heavily in R&D for future growth (by the way, it is very, very easy to pretend this is the case – be warned!).*
○ *If overheads go down too much you might not have the required level of staff to achieve your sales.*

○ *However, as the sales grow, profits are generated by holding overheads at the same level.*

Again, there are no easy answers but these are the things to consider *now* when doing the budget, not later when the fan is dripping with you know what!

" *These guys are always trying to get their budgets through just by jacking up sales and adding loads of new costs. I have to tell them to get real or get out.* "
– Alan Stern, financial director

The basics of planning and budgeting

1. Budgets are essential to plan for an uncertain future.
2. Budgets look at projected sales, costs and investments.
3. Determine how many of each product you can sell at each price.
4. Work out how much you need to sell to break even.
5. Use the budget to manage costs.
6. Resist the temptation to put the projected sales up to make a venture work. Always be realistic.

What's in this chapter for you

> *Understanding investment appraisal*
> *Working out when an investment will pay back*
> *Time is money*

❝ *We keep on buying new kit and being sure that it is just what we need. Then we run into trouble. It doesn't pay its way. We never seem to get it right.* ❞
— **Kenny Doogan, graphic designer**

> How often do you ignore good ideas because you can't calculate whether they will work financially?

Capital investment appraisal

For all companies, the decision to make a major investment can be particularly daunting. For small businesses, it's even worse because it could well break the company. The trick is to do the homework: look dispassionately at any idea and test it to the point where you will know pretty accurately it's chances of success.

Let's look again at the assumptions and P&L for Bertie's New World Direct business:

- ○ *The cost of importing will be 6.00 per bottle for 12,000 and goes down by 1.00 for each additional thousand up to 15,000.*
- ○ *He will need to spend 10,000 on brochures and the same again on mailing them.*
- ○ *Overnight deliveries on the lorry would cost 400 per month.*
- ○ *Mail deliveries will be 100 per month.*
- ○ *He will need a packing person, a driver and a marketing manager at 30,000 per year.*
- ○ *Additional light, electricity and other costs will be 5,000 per year.*

Based on these assumptions, Bertie drew up the following P&L for the first year of his new venture.

Sales		119,850
Cost of sales		
Opening stock	0	
Purchases	60,000	
Closing stock	15,000	
Cost of goods sold		45,000
Gross profit		74,850
Overheads		
Advertising	20,000	
Salaries	30,000	
Light etc.	5,000	
Mail	1,200	
Van deliveries	4,800	
		61,000
Net profit		13,850

> The P&L forecast does not of course take account of the major expenditure on the new machinery and lorry. Why not?

As you well know by now, the lorry and other assets of the direct mail company now become Bertie's assets and go on to his balance sheet, not the P&L. But, you ask, aren't they the major costs associated with the venture? Indeed they are, and to have a true picture of the viability of the project we have to look at when Bertie might get his money back on the new equipment. After all, we know from earlier chapters that the cash and balance sheet implications of a decision can have far more impact than a simple profit and loss.

What's more, Bertie, for all his knowledge and entrepreneurial flair, does not have a cool 45k lying around and has to make a case to the bank manager or to outside investors. They will want to know *when* the money invested will show a return.

Payback

> ❝ *For us it's all about time. We can't have money tied up for ever in exotic hardware. We need results **now**.* ❞
> **– Kenny Doogan**

Payback looks at how long it will take for the initial cash investment in a new asset to be recouped. It focuses on cash flow not sales income.

What will Bertie's first year cash flow look like?

His life is made easier by the fact that all sales are cash sales but on the other hand his importers also demand payment on receipt of goods. Working out how much stock he will need to buy he forecasts cash flows from the new venture as:

Yr 1	–1,150
Yr 2	20,000
Yr 3	30,000
Yr 4	33,000
Yr 5	36,000

So the project pays back in just under three years. In other words he has recouped his cash investment in the new assets with cash received from making those assets work.

❑ *Now does this look a good project?*
❑ *How would you assess it?*

To decide whether the project is a good one we have to look at all our measures together:

- ○ *Is the project profitable?*
- ○ *Does it generate positive cash flows?*
- ○ *When does it pay back?*

In general any payback which takes over four years is probably too long. In that period surely something with a better and quicker return could be done with the money.

Payback 2

Bertie is now so successful he needs better systems. He started off using a very nice but rather old book-keeper. The auditors were somewhat rude about the state of his records and suggested it would be cheaper and more efficient to use a computer system. He looks around and finds one with accounting software for 1,750. He can now let the book-keeper (who was charging 10 per hour for 3 hours a week) go.

What is the payback on the computer?

You might think this is an unfair question as the computer generates no sales, but it does save money. At 30 per week (i.e. the book-keeper's fee) the computer will take 1,750/30 or 58 weeks to pay back which is probably acceptable.

> **"** *We are in an industry where we are always getting new technology thrust at us and are told it will save time or money. We have to be able to measure if this is true and payback is the perfect method.* **"**
> **– Alan Sappstone, Precision Parts**

Payback can be applied to the cash flows generated by a fixed assets or the savings made. Either way it has to be possible to work out the material benefit of something before buying it.

Time is money

If you are really smart you are shaking your head now and thinking "but surely money in three years' time is worth less than money today – at least I could stick it in the bank and earn interest." And you would of course be *RIGHT*.

How would you compensate for the effects of inflation in your cash flow projections?

There is a method for working out the value today of cash flow in the future using the interest rate. For example, 100 today at interest of 10% would be 110 in one year; in two years the 110 would be 121. Another way of looking at it is that 121 in two years' time is only worth 100 today as we could make it 121 just by leaving it in the bank for two years.

There is a simple formula to use when making such calculations:

$$Present\ value = future\ sum \div (1 + r)^n$$

where *r* is the percentage rate of interest expressed as a decimal (so 10% would be 0.1) and *n* is the number of years. So, at an interest rate of 10%, for Bertie's 20,000 in year two:

$$20,000 \div (1.1)^2 = 16,529$$

and the 30,000 in year three is:

$$30,000 \div (1.1)^3 = 22,539$$

and so on.

The payback period becomes more like four years. Whether this is a better method of assessing new investments than straight payback is a matter of some debate. What interest rate do you pick? Bertie wouldn't actually put the money in a bank so it is an unreal comparison. But at least you can talk about *discounted cash flow* and *net present value* now without being bamboozled – because this is all it is!!

> ❝ *Our business is all about the future. We are investing for tomorrow. We need to know what tomorrow will be worth.* ❞
> **– John Hall, Hall's Dreamworks Software**

TIPS ✓

The basics of assessing investments

1. Capital expenditure is money spent on new fixed assets and so appears on the balance sheet.
2. Investment appraisal should always be used to work out the return on a new investment.
3. Use "payback" to tell you how long an asset will take to pay for itself either in sales or savings.
4. Remember: time is money. The value of cash will fall over time.

REMEMBER: none of what has been covered in this book will help you have a great idea or implement it well! However, the techniques described are integral in supporting good business and marketing skills, but don't replace them. Use them wisely and you will be a better business person.